THE POWER OF THOUGHT CHILDREN'S BOOK SERIES

I CAN GROUND MYSELF

Written by Amber Raymond & Lynn McLaughlin

Illustrated by Allysa Batin

Copyright © 2023 by Amber Raymond and Lynn McLaughlin,
in Canada

All rights reserved. No part of this book may be reproduced in any form or by an electronic or mechanical means, including information storage and retrieval systems, without written permission in writing from the copyright owners except by a reviewer who may quote brief passages in a review.

Illustrated by Allysa Batin

ISBN: 978-1-7388582-3-1 (paperback)
ISBN: 978-1-7388582-4-8 (ebook)

https://lynnmclaughlin.com
https://www.messsmakers.com

We all feel many emotions. The characters on the planet Tezra glow in the following colours to match how they are feeling.

Red	Orange	Blue	Yellow	Green	Purple
Anger	Scared	Sad	Surprised	Happy	Lonely
Frustration	Worried	Disappoint-ed	Unexpected Event	1 Believe in Myself	
	Uncertain				

Are You Up For A Challenge?

- Can you see when each character's feelings are changing?
- Can you tell by the look on their faces, by body language or the words they are using? Maybe you can tell by the colour of their glow.
- Have you ever felt the same way? How do you express your own feelings?

"I know we're all **excited**. It's important for us to stick together so everyone is safe. We don't want one of you to get lost or hurt, do we?" Trine said.

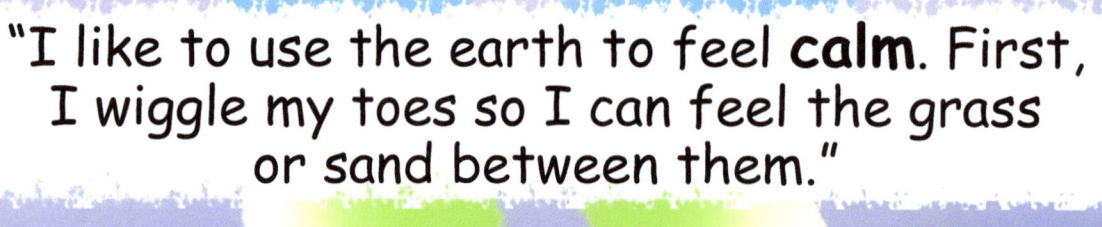

"I like to use the earth to feel **calm**. First, I wiggle my toes so I can feel the grass or sand between them."

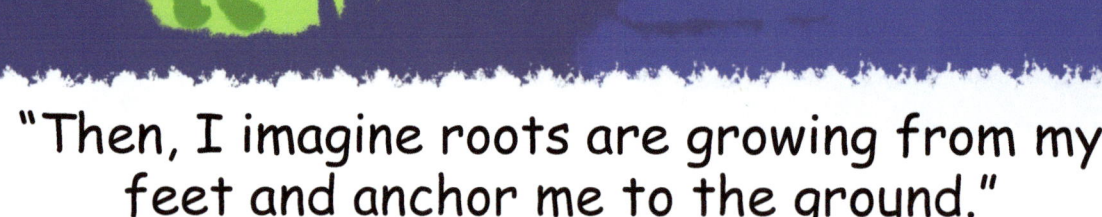

"Then, I imagine roots are growing from my feet and anchor me to the ground."

"I think about my legs turning into the trunk of a tree. I always see really bright colours when that happens," laughed Zirco.

"Then, I imagine my whole body turning into a big tree and I have colourful flowers that grow from my fingers. I can always hear my thoughts better when I connect with the earth."

"Working with the air helps me focus and **calm** myself."

"First, I close my eyes, and put my hands on my belly. I imagine there's a green balloon inside of me that grows and shrinks when I breathe in and out," said Epido with a smile.

"First, I imagine a campfire in front of me. I love the smell of campfires. I focus on the flames until my heartbeat slows down. I feel **peaceful** when my heart is **calm**."

"Then, I think of a place where I feel safe, **calm**, **relaxed** and **happy**. I imagine my own planet and everything I love is there."

When we are **excited**, sometimes we have trouble controlling our emotions.

You Can Use the Elements Too!

1. Notice you are excited or full of emotions by listening to your body.

2. Choose your favourite element to try.

3. Use your imagination to follow the steps for that element.

4. Notice if you are feeling calmer by listening to your body.

5. If you are still too excited or full of emotions, try another element.

Vocabulary

Imagine - to create a picture in our mind of something we want to experience

Earth - parts of nature connected to the ground (e.g. dirt, roots, trees, plants, salt …)

Air - parts of nature that we can breathe (e.g. wind, smells …)

Water - liquid parts of nature (e.g. ocean, lakes, rivers, creeks, ice, baths and showers ...)

Flames - the glowing part of a fire (e.g. candles, campfires ...)

Like You, Every Crystal is Unique!

Did you notice the characters are all named after crystals?

Some crystals look like simple rocks, and others look like they're from another planet. No matter their appearance, they all make you feel a sense of wonder when you see the way they shine.

Also known as rocks, gemstones, and minerals, crystals are formed through geological processes by heat and pressure underground. Working with crystals can help you transform into the most powerful version of yourself by guiding you to see how incredible you truly are.

Carnelian (*Carnuli*): empowerment, focus, action and confidence

Citrine (*Trine*) empowerment, confidence, creativity, manifestation and abundance

Lapis Lazuli (*Lazu*): intuition, education, communication and problem solving

Sardonyx (*Nyx*): empowerment, confidence, leadership, courage, growth and boundaries

Zircon (*Zirco*) : Confidence, wisdom, love and happiness

Epidote (Epido): energize, healthy, strengthen, provide hope, opens you to love and joy

Amber Raymond
MSW, RSW, BSW, BA

WWW.MESSSMAKERS.COM

As a Masters-level Social Worker, Amber is an advocate for unconventional, evidence-based coping strategies and is devoted to her friends and family.

She is passionate about child mental health, lifelong self-care practices, self-exploration, self-love, and holistic wellbeing.

When not practicing social work, Amber likes to research new, effective methods to overcoming life's mental and emotional challenges.

Lynn McLaughlin
MED, BED, BA

WWW.LYNNMCLAUGHLIN.COM

Lynn McLaughlin served as a Superintendent of Education, Administrator and Teacher. Lynn continues to be active in education, teaching future Educational Assistants and working with parent/community groups.

Lynn hosts the inspirational podcast "Taking the Helm" which can be found on VoiceAmerica Radio or on your favourite podcast app.

As a best-selling, award-winning author, and Rotarian, Lynn is dedicated to community causes and volunteerism.

Allysa Batin

Allysa Batin is a young freelance illustrator. She enjoys creating fun and colourful characters and advocating for love and acceptance in her art.

She's happy to spread positivity through the book series, and hopes to continue illustrating in the future.

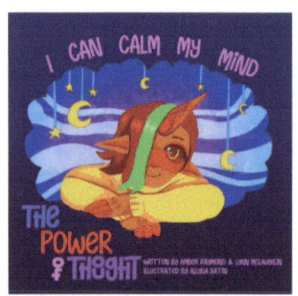
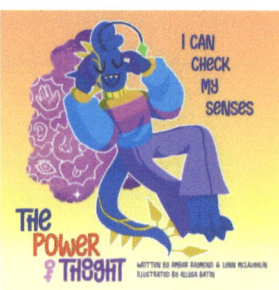

What other adventures do these friends find themselves in?

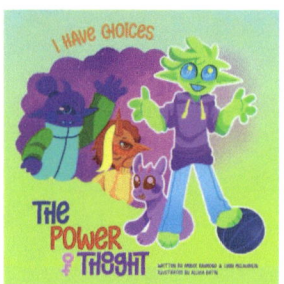

Curious to learn more about emotional well-being? Sign up for your free guide and receive our monthly updates at *www.lynnmclaughlin.com*